Biomes
of the World

DESERT

EDWARD R. RICCIUTI

BENCHMARK BOOKS

MARSHALL CAVENDISH
NEW YORK

Benchmark Books
Marshall Cavendish Corporation
99 White Plains Road
Tarrytown, New York 10591-9001

Series created by Blackbirch Graphics, Inc.

Printed and bound in Hong Kong.

Library of Congress Cataloging-in-Publication Data

Ricciuti, Edward R.
    Desert / Edward R. Ricciuti.
       p.   cm. — (Biomes of the world)
    Includes bibliographical references (p.   ) and index.
    Summary: Describes the earth's desert regions and the plants and
animals that inhabit them.
    ISBN 0-7614-0134-2 (lib. bdg.)
    1. Desert ecology—Juvenile literature. 2. Deserts—Juvenile literature.
[1. Deserts. 2. Desert ecology. 3. Ecology.] I. Title. II. Series.
QH541.5.D4R535   1996
574.5'2652—dc20   95-41070
                                                 CIP
                                                 AC

Contents

Introduction

People traveling in an airplane often marvel at the patchwork patterns they see as they look down on the land. Fields, forests, grasslands, and deserts, each with its own identifiable color and texture, form a crazy quilt of varying designs. Ecologists—scientists who study the relationship between living things and their environment—have also observed the repeating patterns of life that appear across the surface of the earth. They have named these geographical areas biomes. A biome is defined by certain environmental conditions and by the plants and animals that have adapted to these conditions.

The map identifies the earth's biomes and shows their placement across the continents. Most of the biomes are on land. They include the tropical rainforest, temperate forest, grassland, tundra, taiga, chaparral, and desert. Each has a unique climate, including yearly patterns of temperature, rainfall, and sunlight, as well as certain kinds of soil. In addition to the land biomes, the oceans of the world make up a single biome, which is defined by its salt-water environment.

Looking at biomes helps us understand the interconnections between our planet and the living things that inhabit it. For example, the tilt of the earth on its axis and wind patterns both help to determine the climate of any particular biome.

The climate, in turn, has a great impact on the types of plants that can flourish, or even survive, in an area. That plant life influences the composition and stability of the soil. And the soil, in turn, influences which plants will thrive. These interconnections continue in every aspect of nature. While some animals eat plants, others use plants for shelter or concealment. And the types of plants that grow in a biome directly influence the species of animals that live there. Some of the animals help pollinate plants. Many of them enrich the soil with their waste.

Within each biome, the interplay of climatic conditions, plants, and animals defines a broad pattern of life. All of these interactions make the plants and animals of a biome interdependent and create a delicate natural balance. Recognizing these different relationships and how they shape the natural world enables us to appreciate the complexity of life on Earth and the beauty of the biomes of which we are a part.

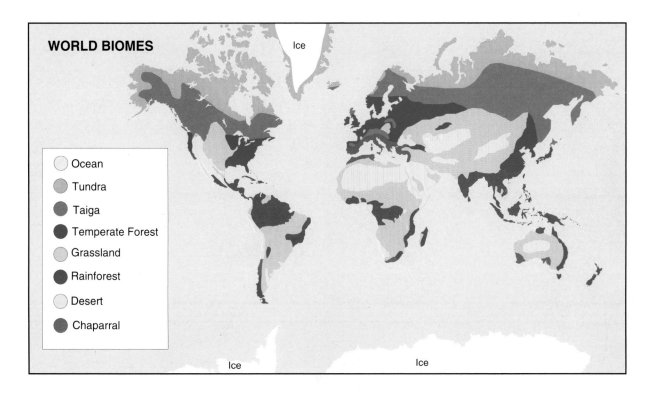

WORLD BIOMES

Ice

- Ocean
- Tundra
- Taiga
- Temperate Forest
- Grassland
- Rainforest
- Desert
- Chaparral

Ice

Ice

1

A Parched World

A narrow ribbon of asphalt known as the Pan-American Highway runs along the rugged seacoast through Peru and Chile. The entire coast of Peru is a desert region called the Costa. Traveling south past Lima, Peru, the highway passes through a desert landscape dotted with huge sand dunes hundreds of feet high. To the east rise the foothills of the Andes Mountains. As one approaches the border with Chile, the desert becomes even more barren. As ocean waves crash on cliffs a stone's throw away, blinding clouds of sand swirl across the road, sometimes piling up like snowdrifts on a winter's day. This is the edge of the driest region on Earth, the Atacama Desert, which lies mostly in Chile but whose northern fringes reach into Peru. Rainfall is so sparse in the Atacama that it can hardly be recorded. In fact, there are places in this desert where rain has never been recorded.

Opposite:
The Atacama Desert in South America is the driest desert on Earth.

7

Deserts of the World

The desert is a biome that takes up some 8.6 million square miles (22 million square kilometers), or more than 5 percent, of the planet's land surface. Scientists define a desert as a place that receives less than 10 inches (25 centimeters) of rain yearly. The Atacama is one of the Earth's driest deserts. As the Atacama demonstrates, rainfall in a desert can be well below 1 inch (2.5 centimeters) annually. Most of the rain that does fall comes during the short rainy seasons, which may be only a few weeks long.

The major North American deserts are the Sonoran, Mojave, Great Basin, and Chihuahua. In addition to the Atacama region, South America has deserts in the portion of Argentina called Patagonia. The Australian desert is made up of several small deserts that merge together, including the Great Sandy and the Great Victoria. Almost all of the Arabian Peninsula is taken up by desert. This Arabian Desert extends northward into Syria; and the Negev desert region of Israel is considered a branch of the Arabian. Two large deserts, the Takla Makan and the Gobi, lie near each other in Central Asia and are often referred to by the name Gobi alone. Africa's great deserts include the Danakil of Ethiopia, the Kalahari of southwestern Africa, and the Sahara, which covers almost the entire northern quarter of the continent.

The largest desert is the Sahara, which covers 3.5 million square miles (9 million square kilometers). The Australian deserts extend for 1.3 million square miles (3.4 million square kilometers). Other large deserts include the Arabian, at nearly 1 million square miles (2.6 million square kilometers), and the Gobi of Asia, at 500,000 square miles (1.3 million square kilometers).

What Makes a Desert?

Several climatic conditions, either alone or in combination, can create a desert. The largest deserts in the world, such as the Sahara, the Arabian, and the Australian, lie

SHAPING SAND DUNES

For dunes to form, a large amount of loose sand must be present. It is the winds, however, that shape them. More specifically, it is the direction and the force of the winds that largely determine the particular shape of a dune. Huge longitudinal dunes—200 miles (322 kilometers) long, 150 feet (46 meters) high, and 2 miles (3 kilometers) wide—form parallel to a strong prevailing wind. Transverse dunes build up at right angles to the prevailing wind, especially where there is a good supply of sand. Crescent-shaped, or barchan, dunes form ahead of the prevailing wind. Winds that blow from several directions can build dunes shaped like pinwheels, or stars.

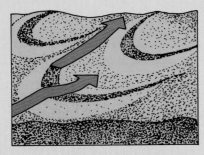

Crescent Dunes
The tips of U-shaped, crescent dunes point in a downwind direction.

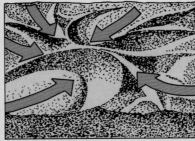

Star-Shaped Dunes
When the wind frequently changes direction, star-shaped dunes are created.

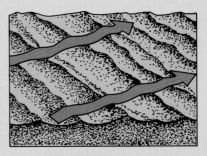

Transverse Dunes
Transverse dunes form at right angles to the prevailing wind.

between latitude 30° South and latitude 30° North. This latitude belt is characterized by virtually constant high-pressure air masses, which keep out the low-pressure masses that bring moisture-laden clouds.

Part of the deserts of the southwestern United States, such as the Mojave and the Great Basin, are created by what is called a rain shadow on mountains. These regions are sheltered from rain-bearing winds moving east from the Pacific Ocean by mountains, particularly the Sierra Nevada. As the winds move up and over the mountains, they cool and drop their moisture. By the time they cross the mountains, they are dry. The areas immediately east of the mountains lie in their rain shadow.

Other deserts, such as the Atacama, are created by ocean currents. In the Pacific Ocean, off the western coasts of Peru and Chile, is the cold Humboldt Current. Winds blowing across the ocean toward shore hold large amounts of moisture, but they lose it as they pass over the cold waters of the current.

However a desert is formed, a lack of cloud cover, almost constant sunny weather, and wind cause whatever rainfall or condensation there is to evaporate quickly. This creates increasing dryness, or aridity.

Different Deserts

Most deserts are very hot. The temperature in Death Valley, which is in the Mojave Desert, has reached as high as 190°F (88°C). However, some deserts can get quite cold during part of the year. An example of a cold desert is the Great Basin Desert, much of which is at a high altitude. Winters bring very cold temperatures, often well below freezing. Because temperatures in the Great Basin Desert and the mountains to the west do not differ in the winter as much as they do in the summer, the westerly winds sometimes bring moisture in the form of snow. Another very cold desert is the Gobi, which, like the Great Basin, is a region of high altitude.

Even hot deserts can be cold at night. Temperatures in the Sahara Desert can soar well over 100°F (38°C) during the day and fall to below freezing after dark. Because the sky is so clear over the Sahara, heat accumulated during the day dissipates very quickly once the sun goes down.

The desert landscape can vary a great deal. Sand, of course, covers large expanses of desert, often piling up into mountainous dunes. In some areas, however, winds blow the sand away, uncovering bare rock. Deserts also have flat areas in which mineral salts accumulate or that are covered with

A layer of snow covers cacti and other plants in an Arizona desert in February.

stones and gravel. Scattered throughout deserts are the beds
of vanished lakes, called playas, the Spanish word for "beaches."
Some deserts, such as those of the southwestern United
States, are mountainous. The deserts have interesting land-
scapes with caves, craggy peaks, and deep canyons.

Huge sand dunes in the Namib Desert drift down to the edge of the Atlantic Ocean in southern Africa.

Deserts sometimes lie side by side with other biomes. Near Las Vegas, Nevada, Mount Charleston rises almost 12,000 feet (3,660 meters) from the desert floor. Atop Mount Charleston grow green forests of ponderosa pine and other coniferous trees. From the sunny, warm city of Las Vegas, during the winter and spring, snow can be seen on the mountaintop, shining white in the sun. Travelers driving north through the desert in southern Peru can look west and watch great flocks of seabirds wheeling and diving into the ocean in search of anchovies and other small fish. In the narrow Gulf of Aqaba, at the northern end of the Red Sea, tourists can go diving and watch colorful coral-reef fish just a few yards offshore. A surfacing diver can look around and see an entirely different world—the desert mountains of southern Israel, Jordan, and Saudi Arabia, bare rocks that loom over the edge of the sea.

The Lively World of the Desert

Deserts, with their extreme temperatures, aridity, poor food resources, and little shelter from the sun and the wind, are harsh places to live. A desert under the midday sun can seem lifeless, but there is more there than often meets the eye. Deserts are home to many plants and animals that have adapted to their difficult living conditions. They have done so by adapting both their bodies and their behaviors.

Animals must keep their bodies from becoming too hot or too cold. This is easiest for mammals and birds. Their body temperatures remain stable as long as they are not exposed to prolonged heat and are able to get enough food to make energy when it is very cold. The body temperature of reptiles and amphibians, however, depends on the animals' surroundings. When a reptile's environment is cold, the reptile is, too. When its surroundings are hot, so is the reptile. A body temperature higher than 104°F (40°C) can kill a reptile, and temperatures on the desert floor often rise far above that level.

Many desert reptiles and other animals protect themselves from temperature extremes by spending much of the time in burrows, where the temperature is more stable than it is at the surface. A burrow can be much cooler than the desert surface in the heat of the day, and warmer during the cold of the night. Still, burrows are used mainly as shelters against the sun. The animals that live in them come out during the cool early morning or evening. In fact, a great many desert animals are active only at night, which is one reason that a desert can seem so lifeless during the day.

Because night temperatures are cooler, nocturnal activity protects animals not only from overheating but also from losing water by evaporation from perspiring. Burrows also help desert animals conserve moisture. A number of these animals spend the driest, hottest times of the year there or in other underground hiding places. During these periods, their body functions slow down—as those of animals that hibernate

THE SECRET OF THE CAMEL'S HUMP

There are two species of camel: the two-humped, or Bactrian camel, and the one-humped, or dromedary. Both are well adapted to the desert and can survive for more than two weeks without water and little, if any, food. Many stories have been told about people lost in the desert who killed camels and drank the water supposedly stored in their stomachs. These stories have no basis in fact.

The contents of the camel's hump—or humps—may be why it can last about ten times longer than a person can without food or water in the blazing desert sun. The hump contains large amounts of fat, which the camel uses for energy when food is not available. When fat is converted to energy, the hydrogen that the fat contains combines with oxygen inhaled through air, to make water. Some scientists think that this is how the camel is supplied with water when there is none to drink. However, a camel that inhales must also exhale, which causes water to evaporate. Therefore, the ability of a camel to survive without much water may actually be due to a number of other things. For example, the blood of a camel holds water longer than does that of a person. Moreover, camels begin to perspire at higher temperatures than people do, and perspiring is an important cause of water loss. What is certain is that when camels are deprived of food and water for a long period of time, their humps shrink.

A Bactrian camel uses the fat in its humps for energy and water. These humps will shrink if a camel goes without food or water for very long.

A desert pocket mouse uses its burrow to escape the very high, daytime temperatures of the Sonoran Desert.

during the winter do—and they need little energy. This process is called estivation. Several types of desert plants also conserve moisture and energy by slowing down growth for most of the year. Many even lack leaves for months at a time. When the brief rains come, these plants burst into life, growing leaves and flowers. At such times, the desert can turn into a garden of green, yellow, red, and many other colors.

Most desert animals and plants have adaptations that conserve water. Some plants, such as cacti, store water in their tissues. Some animals, kangaroo rats among them, get water from the food they eat.

The adaptations that enable plants and animals to survive in the desert are many, and they differ according to each organism's lifestyle. What they all have in common, however, is that they contribute to survival in a biome that most living things could not tolerate for long.

2

A Thin Skin of Plants

The Sonoran Desert is home to a cactus called the saguaro. This cactus begins as a tiny seed that drops from a small, prickly, red fruit. Most saguaro seeds do not survive. They are eaten by such animals as birds and rodents. Those that are not eaten may be parched by the heat of the sun. Those seeds that do survive can grow into a plant that weighs 10 tons (9 metric tons) and grows to a height of 50 feet (15 meters), a giant among cacti. The saguaro is among the many plants that are able to survive in deserts and that, though widely scattered, cover many parts of the biome like a thin skin.

**Opposite:
The adaptations
of a saguaro
cactus help it to
survive in the
desert biome.**

How a Saguaro Survives

The saguaro cactus is one example of the ways in which desert plants have adapted to very specific conditions in order to survive. It grows on rocky and gravelly soils, usually between altitudes of 2,000 to 3,500 feet (610 to 1,068 meters). The southern part of the Sonoran Desert has very hot summers and slightly cool winters. The northern part has hot summers and can experience fairly cold weather in the winter. Saguaros in the southern part of the desert tend to grow on slopes that face the north, and are cooler. Those in the northern part of the desert usually grow on slopes that face the south, where they are shielded from the cold.

Saguaros must take advantage of every bit of moisture in their surroundings. Their roots extend only a few inches in the soil, which allows them to soak up surface moisture from dew and rain before it evaporates. The larger an area the roots cover, the more water they are able to absorb. A fully grown saguaro may be encircled by a root network that reaches 50 feet (15 meters).

Other adaptations help a saguaro absorb and store water. Its tissues are spongy, and its surface is pleated, like the bellows of an accordion. As the cactus fills with water, its trunk and branches swell, to make room for the absorbed water. During a heavy rain, a giant saguaro may absorb up to a ton of water. About 90 percent of the total weight of a saguaro is water.

Slow growth is typical of desert plants. At thirty years, a saguaro is only a few feet high. At about eighty years, it rises 20 feet (6 meters) above the desert floor. Two centuries will pass before it reaches its full height. This slow growth requires less energy and, therefore, less food and water—another plus in the desert.

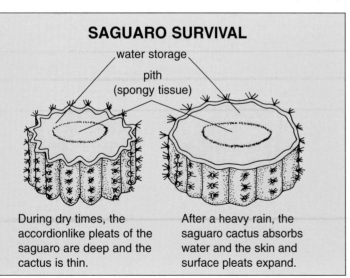

SAGUARO SURVIVAL

water storage

pith
(spongy tissue)

During dry times, the accordionlike pleats of the saguaro are deep and the cactus is thin.

After a heavy rain, the saguaro cactus absorbs water and the skin and surface pleats expand.

SOMETHING FOR ALMOST EVERYONE

During May and June, the saguaro cactus blooms with large, cream-colored flowers, each of which lives for only twenty-four hours. Hummingbirds and doves drink the flowers' nectar during the day, and long-nosed bats and many insects drink it at night. Pollen from the flowers sticks to these creatures, and they carry it to other saguaro blossoms, thus fertilizing them. The fruit that arises from the flowers is eaten by many animals, including peccaries, mule deer, bighorn sheep, rodents, foxes, skunks, and coyotes. Since ancient times, Native Americans have also used the saguaro fruit as food.

The saguaro provides many desert animals not only with food but with homes and nest sites. Hawks and thrashers build nests in the cacti. Woodpeckers drill holes into them and set up house. Several other birds, such as sparrow hawks and elf owls, nest in the holes after the woodpeckers abandon them. As far as desert dwellers go, the saguaro seems to have something for almost everyone.

Saguaro cacti provide food and shelter for many desert animals. Here, a woodpecker brings food for its young back to their cactus nest.

Storing Water

Many other sizable cacti with thick stems and pulpy interiors, such as the barrel and the organ-pipe cacti, are known for storing large amounts of water. As with the saguaro, however, the water is not pooled within the cactus but is absorbed by its tissues. There are many stories about people lost in the desert surviving on water from the barrel cactus. The truth is that the only moisture available from the cactus is a bitter liquid that must be wrung from its pulp with considerable effort.

A group of six adults holding hands can stretch only halfway around the trunk of this massive baobab tree. Its soft-tissue trunk holds moisture, which the tree uses to survive in the arid desert.

Cacti are not the only desert plants with spongy interiors for holding moisture. Among the many others are the euphorbias of Africa, which closely resemble cacti on the outside as well as on the inside. However, cacti and euphorbias are not related. Another is the African baobab tree, whose massive trunk is filled with soft tissue.

Water Conservation

Large amounts of water escape from plants through their leaves. Acacia trees and shrubs, which grow in many deserts, shed their leaves during the long, dry periods. So does the ocotillo, an American desert shrub.

Desert plants that lose their leaves and seem dead for much of the year come alive as soon as the rains arrive. Two or three days after a heavy downpour, the ocotillo plant is covered with new leaves. Being without leaves during the dry season not only prevents water from escaping but also slows growth and, thus, the plant's need for moisture.

A vast number of desert plants spend most of their existence as seeds, which can survive without a water supply. They sprout only after rainwater pene- trates the soil and reaches them. Some scientists believe that rainwater washes away chemicals in the seeds' coats that prevent them from sprouting. Even if they are wet, however, these seeds will not sprout during seasons when tempera- tures are very high or very low. Sprouting during moderate weather increases the chances of the plants' survival. All of their growth—and need for water—is packed into one short burst of life. Many such plants grow, flower, and go to seed within two months, or sometimes less.

The agaves are plants of the North American deserts that bloom just once every seven to twenty years. It was long believed that these plants flowered only once in a century, and for this reason agaves are also known as century plants. The different species of century plants

An agave's tall flower stalk rises from a base of pointy leaves. The agave blooms only once every seven to twenty years.

The spiny leaves of these Joshua trees protect them from the hot desert sun and help retain moisture.

range from small ones with leaves only a few inches long to big ones with leaves several feet long. The leaves, which are long and pointed, grow in a low clump on the ground. As blooming time approaches, a flower stalk rises from the middle of the clump. The flower stalks of the agave can grow at a rate of more than a foot a day and reach a height of 20 feet (6 meters). After the agave blooms, the flower dies, leaving behind its seeds.

The shape and the structure of the leaves of many desert plants reduce their rate of water loss. On many Asian deserts, the small saxaul tree is a common plant. This tree's leaves are so narrow that they provide no shade for a person sitting underneath the tree. The leaf's small surface area reduces the amount of moisture that can escape. Tough, waxy coverings on such plants as yuccas also slow water loss. A large yucca called the Joshua tree is among those desert plants covered with thick coats of spines or hair, which insulate the plants against the heat of the sun and help hold in moisture.

Some desert plants protect themselves from the heat and conserve moisture by growing almost entirely underground. A number of plants related to one another in southern Africa expose only a portion of their leaves above the surface. They are often mistaken for rocks and pebbles and, in fact, are called living stones.

Tapping Underground Water

Although the surface of a desert may be dry as a bone, there may be water deep beneath it. Water seeps through the soil from higher elevations, and underground streams may flow from caves and hidden springs. Most desert plants cannot make use of this water. Some, though, can tap this life-giving water source with roots that drill deep into the earth. The roots of the mesquite tree, which grows in American deserts, can extend 100 feet (30.5 meters) deep, while those of the acacia tree can penetrate dozens of feet below the surface. Desert trees, including the mesquite and the catclaw, often grow most thickly in and along gullies and dry riverbeds that fill with water only during infrequent cloudbursts. Often, water trickles

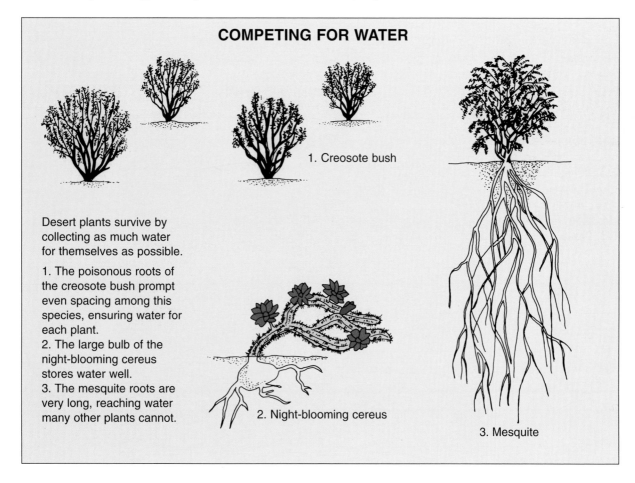

COMPETING FOR WATER

Desert plants survive by collecting as much water for themselves as possible.

1. The poisonous roots of the creosote bush prompt even spacing among this species, ensuring water for each plant.
2. The large bulb of the night-blooming cereus stores water well.
3. The mesquite roots are very long, reaching water many other plants cannot.

1. Creosote bush

2. Night-blooming cereus

3. Mesquite

through the soil far below these places, where the deep-drilling roots of these trees can reach it.

Sagebrush, which grows in deserts in western North America, has a built-in suction pump with which it obtains water. By closing and opening pores in its leaves, the plant creates a pump that draws water from the ground into its roots.

Chemical Warfare

A common trait of desert shrubs is that individual plants are spaced widely apart from one another. One reason for this is that there is not enough moisture to support additional plants. However, some scientists suspect that there may be another reason. The roots of some desert plants, such as the creosote bush, produce chemicals that kill other plants that come too close. In this way, they keep intruders away from their source of water.

The roots of the creosote bush release chemicals that keep any other plant from growing too close and, thus, using any available moisture.

FROM TOP TO BOTTOM

Because temperature decreases with altitude, and because the tops of mountains may receive more precipitation than the lowlands, a mountain-top can have a very different environment than that of the desert below. The vegetation atop a mountain may resemble that of regions thousands of miles to the north.

Some mountains that rise in the Arizona desert, for example, are surrounded by such plants as creosote bushes at their bases. As the slope and the elevation increase, groves of saguaro cactus appear. Above about 4,000 feet (1,220 meters), a mixture of oaks and shrubby plants called chaparral emerge. As elevation increases and temperature decreases, pines mix with oaks. Above 7,000 feet (2,135 meters) grow forests of ponderosa pines, such as those that grow at lower elevations in the mountains of northern Nevada and California. At about 9,000 feet (2,745 meters), an entirely new forest takes over. It is made up of fir trees similar to those that grow in the forests as far north as southern Alaska. Finally, at about 11,000 feet (3,355 meters) above the hot desert floor is a forest of firs and spruces, much like the northern coniferous forest that covers vast areas through the centers of Alaska and Canada, from coast to coast. The layering of plant zones on a mountain is called stratification.

Coping with Shifting Sands

Of all the deserts, those covered with sand contain the most vegetation. It is easier for the roots of plants to penetrate sand than hard, rocky soil. However, sand also presents plant roots with a problem. Blown by the wind, desert sands are continuously shifting and moving from one place to another, a process that can uproot plants.

The greatest movement of sand occurs in dune areas, where many desert grasses and sedges grow. These plants, like their relatives that grow on dunes along seashores, have a large network of tough roots that claw into the sand and hold firm. Once the grasses and the sedges are established, they in turn anchor the dunes in place against the force of the wind.

3

The Face of the Desert

The dark of night has fallen over the Namib Desert, which borders the Atlantic Ocean in southwestern Africa. In the blackness, several huge, hulking forms troop out of the sandy wilderness to the seaside shallows. Desert elephants have come to the ocean to bathe. It may seem surprising, but elephants can be counted among the animals that roam the desert. Small numbers of elephants live in the desert of Namibia, which borders South Africa on the northwest. These desert elephants live mostly on palm trees and their fruits. They live in a world of windblown sands, where water holes are few and far between and plants are scarce.

27

Big Beasts

Since desert vegetation is tough, not very nutritious, and thinly scattered, deserts do not support nearly as many large creatures as do grasslands. However, several types of big animals, like elephants, can be numbered among those that inhabit deserts. The large ears of an elephant allow it to lose excess heat. Blood vessels in the ears enlarge and heat then passes out of the blood and skin into the air. Some of the other large creatures, such as lions, do not have any adaptations for life in the desert. Nonetheless, some of them manage to survive in places like the Kalahari Desert of southern Africa. They are

Some large animals are able to adapt to life in the desert. Here, an elephant dusts itself with soil.

A MODEL DESERT ANIMAL

A North American bannertail kangaroo rat rests outside of its burrow.

The little kangaroo rat, which lives in many North American deserts, serves as a model for the way an animal can survive the scarcity of water. Kangaroo rats seldom, if ever, drink. Their diet consists mostly of seeds, although they also eat insects. Food is broken down within a kangaroo rat's body in a way that produces a large amount of water. The rat's kidneys are remarkable. They concentrate urine so that it becomes almost solid, thereby reducing water loss. Kangaroo rats also lack sweat glands, so they do not lose water through evaporation by perspiring. Evaporation also occurs when an animal exhales warm air. However, when the kangaroo rat exhales, its breath is cooled as it passes over the lining of its nasal passages, which reduces evaporation.

Evaporation is one way to stay cool. The kangaroo rat's behavior keeps it from overheating. It lives in a burrow, which it leaves only at night, when the air is a bit more humid and much cooler than it is after the sun rises. Air in a burrow is generally more humid than that aboveground. During the day, the rat remains in its burrow, which it plugs up to prevent the moisture in the burrow from evaporating at the surface.

There lives in Asia and Africa a small rodent that closely resembles the kangaroo rat, and it has similar adaptations for coping with a lack of water. The two animals look almost exactly alike, but they are not closely related. Unrelated animals living in similar conditions in different parts of the world often have similar shapes and exhibit similar behavior.

less concentrated in the desert than on the plains, however, because the antelope and other animals on which they prey are not abundant.

Most desert creatures are of small to medium size. They—rodents and lizards, for instance—belong to groups whose members can be found in other land biomes. They are very similar to their relatives that do not live in the desert and they all share a common need: getting enough moisture in a world almost devoid of water.

Ways to Get Water

A large number of desert animals obtain water from their food. Lizards extract water from insects and plants, desert tortoises get water from cacti and other plants, and roadrunners get it from eating lizards, snakes, insects, and other animals.

Among the antelope that inhabit deserts are the oryx. A type of oryx known as the gemsbok is a major source of food for lions in the Kalahari. Gemsbok use their front feet to dig up a melonlike fruit, the tschamma. The fruit and its roots provide not only food but also moisture for the gemsbok. The endangered Arabian oryx once roamed vast areas of the Middle East but was eventually exterminated in the wild by people. Zoos in many parts of the world have bred this species in captivity, and it has been reintroduced in parts of its former range. The Arabian oryx seems to be able to detect rainfall a long distance away and commonly travels helter-skelter across the desert in search of water. When no water is available, the oryx is able to live for long periods on the moisture it gets from eating melons and similar fruits.

The addax, a close relative of the oryx that inhabits the Sahara, is the antelope best adapted to desert conditions. It seldom, if ever, drinks. Instead, it obtains moisture from the plants on which it feeds. Some scientists believe that pockets on the stomach lining of the addax store water for use when water is not readily available.

Storing Water and Food

Storing water is one way in which many desert creatures survive where it is so scarce. The desert tortoise of western North America has two pouches under its shell that hold water derived from the cacti on which it feeds. When food is plentiful, the Gila monster—a large, venomous lizard—and the Egyptian spiny tailed lizard build up reserves of fat in their thick tails. When food is scarce, they live off of this fat, which

A herd of gemsbok move across the Namib Desert in search of water.

31

also provides moisture. Some desert rodents, such as the kangaroo rat and the pocket mouse, store seeds in their burrows and eat them when they are not available on the surface.

Escaping from the Heat

Keeping cool conserves water in an animal's body. Besides staying in burrows during the hottest hours of the day, desert animals have evolved several different ways of escaping the heat. Addax are active during the cooler parts of day—in the early morning, evening, and after dark. During the hottest hours, however, they lie down in holes that they dig in the sand with their forefeet.

Light colors reflect the rays of the sun, so it is not a coincidence that desert creatures are often pale in color. Some lizards are able to change color in response to different temperatures. In the cool morning, light-colored cells in their skin expand. As the sun, and thus the temperature, rises, these

LOUNGING LIZARDS

Most desert lizards regulate their temperature by taking positions in relation to the sun's rays.

1. Early morning   2. Midmorning   3. Midday

1. A lizard places itself broadside to the sun's rays, warming its body.

2. Hunting takes place midmorning. If a lizard gets too hot, it raises its body and tail off the ground.

3. A lizard takes shelter from the hot midday sun inside its burrow.

4. A lizard becomes active again in the midafternoon.

5. A lizard absorbs the heat of the fading late afternoon sun before returning to its burrow for the night.

4. Midafternoon   5. Late afternoon

cells contract, and the dark-colored cells expand. Many desert reptiles regulate their temperature by taking different positions in relation to the sun's rays.

The flattened shell of the African spurred tortoise creates a large surface that absorbs heat. To cool off, the tortoise faces the sun so that its back is not directly exposed to the rays, and it raises its tail and body off the hot ground. It also digs burrows to avoid the heat. To warm up, a lizard positions itself broadside to the sun, exposing as much of its body as possible and keeping its underparts in contact with the ground. To cool off, it faces the sun so that it is least exposed to the rays, and it raises its body and tail off the ground.

Desert Travel

By looking at the feet of a desert animal, especially a mammal, it is possible to make a good guess about the type of desert in which it lives. The elephants of the Namib Desert have broader feet than do elephants that live elsewhere. The addax has large, spreading hooves. Both animals are adapted for traveling over sand without sinking deeply into it. The African wild ass, which is of the same species as the domestic burro, also has hooves adapted to the desert. The ass lives in a different kind of desert than that inhabited by the addax. It lives in the rough, stony deserts of northern or northeastern Africa. Its hooves, the longest and narrowest of any member of the horse family, are designed to enable the ass to keep its footing among the rocks.

Several hooved mammals that are found in rocky, mountainous areas in other biomes also live in desert mountain ranges. Wild sheep inhabit montane pastures found in North America, Asia, Europe, and northern Africa. A wild goat called the ibex is common in hilly country within African and Asian deserts. Most of these animals, however, are not as well adapted to deserts as the addax and the wild ass are, and they must live within reach of water.

An ibex family climbs on a mountainside in Israel. Their hooves help them to navigate the rocks and crevices.

Prey and Predator

As it does elsewhere in the natural world, survival in the desert depends on finding something to eat and not being eaten. Desert animals have some of the same traits that other creatures rely on to find prey. Since most desert creatures feed by night, they have adaptations that help them hunt for a meal in the dark, when vision is not a key sense. Around the world, there are several different species of desert foxes, which hunt rodents, lizards, insects, and other small creatures. They include the fennec and the bat-eared fox of Africa, the sand fox of Asia, and the kit fox of North America. These foxes have large—huge, even—outer ears, which gather and funnel sounds to the eardrum, helping them to locate prey.

The large ears of a fennec fox help it to get rid of excess heat as well as pick up sounds of potential prey.

Deserts in the Americas are home to several kinds of rattlesnakes, which search for small mammals that come out at night. Rattlesnakes have organs in their snouts that sense odors, such as those given off by a warm-blooded mammal. They use these organs to track prey in the darkness.

Most desert birds are active by day and depend on vision to find their food. Hawks and eagles have excellent vision, both for scanning large expanses of land and for locating individual prey.

WATERBIRDS OF THE DESERT

Ducks, herons, and ibises are all waterbirds, but they—along with several other types of aquatic birds—are also found in deserts. Scattered throughout the world's deserts are places where water wells up from underground springs or trickles down from nearby mountains. Waterbirds often gather in these areas, especially during their migrations. So do many other types of birds, which are drawn by the standing water and the thick vegetation that grows around it.

About 20 miles (32 kilometers) from Las Vegas, Nevada, in the Desert National Wildlife Refuge, lies Corn Creek, 10 acres (4 hectares) of spring-fed ponds surrounded by greenery in an otherwise colorless countryside. Mallards and other ducks dabble in the ponds. White-faced ibises, an unusual sight, wade in the shallows. Coots navigate among water plants. All told, more than 200 species of birds have been seen at Corn Creek. Besides waterbirds, they include western tanagers, yellow-headed blackbirds, and yellow-rumped warblers. Corn Creek is proof that the desert is truly alive with wild creatures.

Desert animals have as many defenses against predators as do animals that inhabit other regions. When targeted as food, the spiny tailed lizard runs for its burrow and dives in, leaving its chunky tail, which is studded with sharp spines, exposed. It swings the tail like a club to ward off its enemies. The ability of many lizards to change their color helps them blend in with their surroundings. This natural camouflage protects them from predators. The kangaroo rat, which is no taller than a person's little finger, has long, powerful hind legs and feet. As its name suggests, it hops like a kangaroo, covering ground at almost 1,200 feet (366 meters) a minute. It uses its long tail, which is tipped with a tuft of hair, as a rudder while it is in the air. The kangaroo rat can make a right-angle turn in mid-jump. This makes it very difficult to catch. If it is able to, the kangaroo rat takes shelter in its burrow, where it joins others in the hidden world of animals, under the face of the desert.

4

The Hidden Desert

Much of the desert's animal life stays out of sight, at least part of the time. None is harder to see than the hordes of small creatures that live amid the sand, rocks, and other materials of the desert's surface and in the soil beneath it. Life also abounds in underground pockets, such as caves and springs. Animals of this hidden desert world include vertebrates—animals with backbones, such as lizards and even fish—and a vast number of invertebrates—animals that do not have backbones, such as spiders and insects.

Spiders and Their Kin

Deserts teem with a group of invertebrates called the arachnids, including spiders and scorpions, which get moisture from fluids in the animals they eat. In deserts from North America to Australia lives a group of spiders called trap-door spiders. They got their name because of the way they catch insects. The trap-door spider lives in a tubelike burrow, which it digs straight down into the ground. It lines the burrow, including the opening, with silk. Then it makes a trapdoor by cutting the silk around the edge of the opening, leaving just enough of it intact to make a hinge. Afterward, the spider camouflages the top of the door with bits of soil, vegetation, and other items. The spider spends most of the time in its burrow,

After sensing the movement of a passing insect, a trap-door spider climbs out of its burrow.

waiting until it senses the movement of an insect passing near the hidden door. When the insect comes close, the spider rushes out, grabs its prey, and hauls it back into its burrow.

Among the other spiders found in deserts are the tarantulas, large, hairy creatures that live in the Americas and the Mediterranean. Some are as big as a person's hand. A similar, but unrelated spider, is the large huntsman spider of Australia. This spider hunts various small creatures, including insects, nestling birds, lizards, and snakes. Tarantulas themselves are the prey of a wasp whose sting paralyzes them.

Although tarantulas look scary and do bite, their poison is not dangerous to people. A few other types of spiders that inhabit deserts, however, are dangerous. These include the black widow and the brown recluse.

Scorpions are another group of arachnids found in deserts. Some scorpions have stings that can be very painful, or even fatal, to humans. Scorpions have large pincers that they use to catch their prey, which consists mostly of insects. Their long, jointed tail is tipped with a curved stinger. The stinger is sometimes used against prey. Usually, however, it is used as a means of self-defense.

Two other groups of arachnids bear a slight resemblance to scorpions and are often mistaken for them. One group is the whip scorpions; the other, the wind scorpions. Many people believe that both groups of spiders are dangerous to humans, but, in reality, they have no stingers. Wind scorpions often burrow in the sand or hide under rocks by day and hunt insects and other small creatures at night.

Arachnids have a covering, known as an exoskeleton, that is thick and hard enough to prevent the escape of moisture from their bodies. This is a great advantage in the desert. Insects also have an exoskeleton, which is why vast numbers of them are able to live in deserts. Insects are most abundant during the periods of greatest plant growth. When the plants die, many adult insects also die, although they have already

GROWING UP FAST

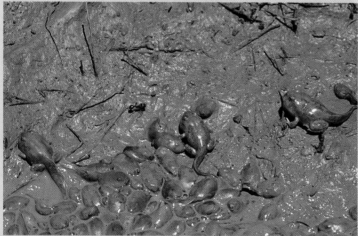

The Great Basin spadefoot toad lives in a desert that is cold during the winter and dry during most of the summer and fall. Toads are amphibians, creatures that cannot tolerate very cold temperatures and need moisture to survive. Spadefoot toads escape the harsh climate by spending much of the year in underground burrows. While in the burrows, body functions slow down, so that little energy is used and the toads can live without eating.

Between April and July, brief but heavy rains come to the Great Basin Desert. When moisture reaches the toads' burrows, the animals come to the surface to mate. Their mating and the development of their young occur during a brief period of time.

When the toads mate, the female releases eggs and the male fertilizes them. Most toad eggs take weeks to hatch. Then the young go through a tadpole stage that lasts for about a month before the tadpoles take on adult form. Spadefoot-toad eggs hatch and tadpoles develop into miniatures of the adults within the space of only a few weeks. These young toads are able to leave the water before the streams and pools dry up. As the dry season continues, all the toads retreat to their burrows to wait for the next rainy season.

The eggs of the spadefoot toad (top) start to develop into tadpoles. As tadpoles (middle), the animals still have tails when they leave the water. In a few weeks, each will look like a miniature adult (bottom).

mated and produced fertilized eggs that will start another generation when the plants once again burst into life.

It is not uncommon for some desert animals to live for only a short while as adults, during which time they mate and leave behind eggs that eventually hatch. Sometimes there may be a span of many years between the time that the adults mate and the time that the eggs hatch. A scientific study done in the Mojave desert provides good evidence for this. In 1955, a dry lake bed was flooded for the first time in a quarter of a century. Almost instantly, the water was crowded with tiny shrimp. These shrimp hatched from eggs that had been laid twenty-five

These young scorpions, seen here on the back of their mother, already have the pincers and curved stingers of adult scorpions.

years earlier, the last time the lake had held water. Over the years, the eggs had held enough moisture to survive. At the touch of water, they burst, releasing a new generation of shrimp. In turn, this new generation would mate, and their fertilized eggs would await the next flood.

Swimming in the Sand

Many desert lizards burrow into the ground, but some actually travel through the sand. The comblike fringe of scales on the toes of the fringe-toed lizard enables it to travel over the surface of the sand as if it were on snowshoes. What is more, with its fringed toes, this lizard can submerge itself in the sand and move through it as though it were swimming.

The fringe-toed lizards have eyelids that overlap, flaps over its ears, and valves that open and close its nostrils—all of which keeps sand out while it is burrowing. Some other

The fringe-toed lizard is able to bury itself in the desert soil and actually travel right through the sand.

The S-shaped movement of the sidewinder protects it from the heat, presenting the least surface area of the rattlesnake to the hot sand.

reptiles, such as the sand skink and the shovel-nosed snake, are also adept at burrowing into the sand and traveling beneath its surface.

The sidewinder rattlesnake travels through loose sand by curving part of its body to form an S-shaped loop. The looped area anchors the snake in place while it pulls the rest of its body forward.

Another snake that is adapted for life in the desert is the sand viper. It conceals itself by coiling its pale-colored body and sinking into the sand until it is partly covered. Because of its position and the color of its body, this snake is very difficult to see.

At Home Underground

Several desert foxes have the ability to burrow deeply into sand. These include the fennec and the bat-eared fox. The little sand fox, which is the size of a large house cat, digs a large system of burrows up to 50 feet (15 meters) long. These burrow systems, each of which houses a single fox family, have several hallways that lead to small chambers, which the foxes line with vegetation. Badgers and skunks are among other medium-size desert mammals that excavate large burrows that they use as underground homes.

Fish in a Dry World

This fact surprises many people, but the list of animals that inhabit deserts includes fish. Many desert fish are confined to tiny areas, such as small river systems or springs. For example, the entire population of the Devil's Hole pupfish, a few hundred in number, lives above a limestone shelf in a spring hole within Death Valley National Monument, in Nevada. All members of this species feed and breed within an area less than 30 square yards (25 square meters). It is the smallest known range of any vertebrate. Another small Nevada fish, the Moapa dace, can be found only within 2 miles

THE NIGHT FLIGHT

Carlsbad Caverns, a huge cave system in New Mexico's Chihuahua Desert, serves as a giant burrow for 300,000 Mexican free-tailed bats that roost there during the day. These bats hang from the ceiling of a part of the caverns called the Bat Cave, which is 200 feet (61 meters) beneath the surface and 600 feet (183 meters) from the entrance. The Bat Cave provides shelter from the day's heat and a place for the female bats to bear and nurse their young. (Each female bat gives birth to one young bat, usually in June.) The roosting bats pack themselves together tightly, so that a single square foot of ceiling can contain 300 of them.

When the sky begins to darken above the desert, the bats on the ceiling begin to move about and stretch their wings. They are preparing to leave their daytime shelter and wing their way over the desert in search of flying insets.

As night approaches, the bats begin to fly toward the entrance and head into the sky, a few at a time. Meanwhile, more and more of those still on the ceiling are milling about. Then, whirling like a tornado, a huge cloud of bats spills from the mouth of the Bat Cave and makes its way through the heavens to nearby river valleys, where their insect prey abounds.

As dawn approaches, the bats go back to the cave. Unlike their mass exit at dusk, their return is quieter. They fly in small groups, even one at a time. High up in the air, each bat folds its wings and falls toward the opening of the cave. As it nears, the bat reopens its wings and flies away from the light of dawn into the darkness of the Bat Cave.

At nightfall, these Mexican free-tailed bats leave their cave by the hundreds of thousands to prey on insects.

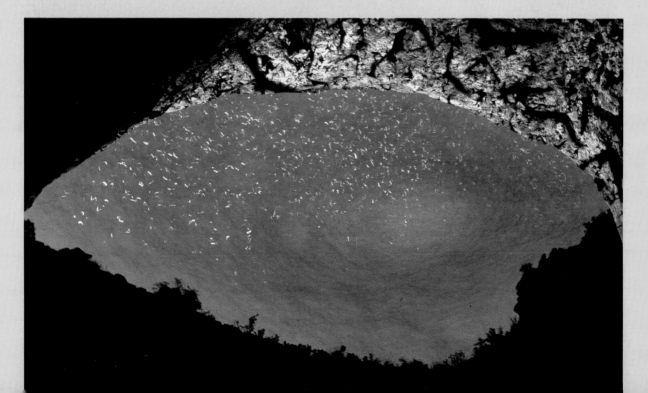

(3 kilometers) of the small stream for which it is named. The Leon Springs pupfish lives only along a single stream system in Pecos County, Texas.

Scientific studies of the deserts of the southwestern United States have found the answer to why many fish living there do so only in isolated pockets. During the last Ice Age, this region's climate was much wetter than today. Permanent

Desert fish are usually confined to tiny areas of water. These Devil's Hole pupfish live in a spring hole in Death Valley, Nevada.

streams flowed through the area. After the end of the Ice Age, the climate became dry and streams disappeared or were broken up into separate sections. The populations of many fish species were cut off from one another. Some vanished. Others interbred and developed into new species with small numbers of individuals. Because they are isolated and have few members, many desert fish species are in danger of extinction.

5

Threats to the Desert

The desert may be a harsh environment, but it is also very fragile and easy to destroy. It can take hundreds, even thousands, of years for a desert to recover from environmental damage. Because of a scarcity of water, desert plants grow very slowly. Some, such as the giant saguaro cactus, need two centuries to reach full size. Thus, an area of desert on which plants have been destroyed will probably remain barren for a very long time. Once plants are gone, desert soils are at the mercy of wind and water. Even in deserts untouched by human activity, soils are loose and easily dispersed. When such activity impinges on vegetation and the soil, the results can be disastrous. It has been calculated, for example, that driving a motorcycle for 1 mile (1.6 kilometers) across the desert may dislodge close to a ton of topsoil. Off-road driving is one example of a human activity that has greatly damaged the desert environment.

Riding Around the Desert

Many types of human activities have harmed deserts. In the California desert, for example, people who engage in unrestricted off-road driving have ruined large tracts of desert. Tracks of all-terrain vehicles and motorcycles crisscross the landscape and may remain etched in the soil for years to come. In some areas, races take place in which more than a thousand motorcycles set off, screaming across the sand. Repeated motor-vehicle traffic has created cuts in the ground several feet deep and has stripped the landscape of vegetation. Without plants, desert animals are deprived of food and shelter. The result is that both plants and animals dwindle in number.

Some conservationists argue that people should not have the right to drive vehicles anywhere they wish in the desert. Although many people enjoy recreation in the desert, they often abuse the privilege. Most conservationists are not seeking to ban off-road driving, but they believe that it should be restricted to certain areas, such as designated trails. On some public desert lands, these sorts of rules are already in effect. For instance, someone driving a four-wheeler off designated areas in the Lake Mead National Recreation Area of Nevada and Arizona is likely to be stopped by a park ranger.

Developing the Desert

Just as people need recreation, they need space on which to build homes and businesses. However, much of the desert is not suitable for development because of its fragile environment. In the southwestern United States, many desert

Building in the desert disrupts the fragile habitats located there. Here, housing developments and businesses lie in a desert canyon in Sedona, Arizona.

Chuckwalla numbers are declining, in part due to the people who take them from the desert to be raised as pets.

regions have attracted large numbers of people who want to live where the weather is sunny for most of the year. Huge housing developments have marched across the land. With people come shopping centers and businesses, which further encroach on the desert. When people pour into the desert, they place a severe strain on the scant water supplies. Many desert streams and springs have been drained to provide water for people, farms, and industries. The great Colorado River, which flows from the Rocky Mountains through the desert southwest into Mexico's Gulf of California, once spread out in broad sheets of water over its delta. So much water has been siphoned from the river, however, that it has been reduced to a mere trickle where it enters the gulf.

In many parts of the world, people have allowed live-stock, such as cattle and goats, to overgraze desert vegetation. This has happened in the United States and in northern Africa. The problem is especially serious in regions where people live in poverty and must use all available resources in order to stay alive. In such places, the gathering of desert vegetation for firewood also damages the environment.

Desert Plants and Animals in Danger

Some species of desert plants and animals are declining because they are especially attractive to people. Many types of rare cacti are sought after by plant fanciers who collect them or use them for landscaping. Entire populations of cacti have been wiped out by collectors. Over the years, there has been a booming trade in cacti, with some unusual species bringing in hundreds of dollars apiece. Moreover, a few desert animals, especially such lizards as the chuckwalla, have been reduced in number by those who collect for the pet trade.

Often, several different human activities combine to place a desert plant or animal in grave danger. The saguaro cactus has been attacked by mining and ranching, which has destroyed countless members of this species. A saguaro seed will not sprout unless it is shaded. When other desert vegetation is eliminated, the number of young saguaros decreases. The saguaro cactus has also been a key target of plant collectors. To add insult to injury, some people find strange enjoyment in chopping off the arms of the cactus.

The desert tortoise of Utah, Nevada, Arizona, and California is another victim of a combination of human activities. Plants used by the tortoise for food and shelter have been reduced by development, off-road driving, and grazing by livestock. Large numbers of tortoises are killed while they are crossing highways. Ravens, which prey on young tortoises, are increasing in number because they find extra food and water around garbage dumps and housing developments.

Nevada's Moapa dace has also been hurt in several ways. The stream in which it lives was diverted for ranching. A resort was built near the springs that give rise to the stream, and its bed was reconstructed in some places with concrete. These and other forms of habitat destruction have reduced the areas in which the fish can breed and feed.

Several species of gazelles from North Africa and the Arabian Desert have also been driven to near extinction because people have hunted them in excessive numbers. Gazelle meat has always been a source of protein for desert peoples. Once modern firearms and motor vehicles became available, however, people had the means with which to kill many more gazelles than they had in the past.

Saving the Desert

Laws have been passed to protect many desert species and the environment on which they depend. Many desert areas have been set aside as parks and preserves. There are now preserves for the desert tortoise, and the U.S. government has purchased the section of stream where most Moapa dace live. A large area of saguaro habitat has also been set aside as a national monument.

THE DESERT BIGHORN

The desert bighorn sheep is a type of bighorn found in the mountains and desert in the southwestern United States and in northern Mexico. Although it is not in danger of extinction, the number of desert bighorn has dwindled in several areas. People have disturbed them and livestock has encroached on much of its food supply.

The U.S. government, however, has established several preserves that protect the desert bighorn's habitat. One is the Desert National Wildlife Range, near Las Vegas, Nevada. It was established in 1936 and covers more than 2,200 square miles (5,698 square kilometers) of the Mojave Desert. The range has major mountains, some rising to almost 10,000 feet (3,050 meters). Vegetation varies from creosote bushes and shrubs on the desert floor to pines atop the mountains.

Although preserving the bighorn's habitat is the main objective of the range, it also provides a home for many other creatures, including 260 species of birds, mule deer, coyotes, bobcats, and mountain lions.

People can use the range as well, for hiking, horseback riding, wildlife watching, and camping. The bighorn sheep are sufficiently numerous that hunting some of them is permitted, under tightly controlled regulations.

The Desert National Wildlife Range in Nevada has been established to protect desert bighorn sheep.

DESERT RESCUE

The Arabian oryx, which became extinct in the wild in 1972, has been reintroduced into its Middle Eastern homeland from animals bred at zoos, mostly in the United States. Since the early 1980s, oryx have been released in Saudi Arabia, Jordan, Oman, and Israel. Their numbers in the wild have increased to more than 300, and zoo herds are also prospering.

The largest concentration of oryx, numbering about 100, is in Jordan, on a preserve. Other herds live in the desolate Empty Quarter of Oman, near Saudi Arabia's Red Sea coastline, and in southern Israel, not far from the city of Elath.

Motor vehicles and machine guns used by British government workers, American oil-company employees, and newly wealthy oil sheiks, spelled the end for the wild oryx in the first half of this century. Wary, tough, and willing to fight with its long horns, the oryx was considered by many Arabs to be a symbol of strength. Traditionally, the power of the oryx was believed to be transferred to the one who killed or ate it, leading to the saying that the oryx is "the doctor of the Arabs."

It was a soldier who, in 1962, led the expedition that captured wild oryx for breeding in zoos. Retired British Army officer Ian Grimwood, then Kenya's chief game warden, caught three oryx in the Arabian Desert.

The animals were sent to the Phoenix Zoo in Arizona, where breeding began.

Operation Oryx, as the reintroduction was first called, has been hailed by the World Wildlife Fund as "one of the most ambitious projects" of its type. It set the stage for reintroductions from zoo stock of other species that have vanished from the wild, such as the black-footed ferret in Wyoming. Planned for the near future are reintroductions that include the California condor.

An oryx grazes undisturbed in an Israeli preserve.

Other laws have been created that prohibit the collecting of certain plant and animal species. These laws have helped, but more are needed, as they do not always work. Because rare species can be sold for considerable sums of money, illegal collecting continues. People can help protect rare desert species by buying only plants that have been raised in green-houses and animals that have been bred in captivity. Some rare desert species, such as the Arabian oryx, have been raised in zoos and released back into the wild.

The desert may seem like a forbidding place at times, but, like the other biomes, it is a key part of life on Earth. Like the other biomes, it must be preserved.

The Saguaro National Monument in Arizona is a protected zone for the plant that is often targeted by collectors and vandals.

Glossary

adaptation A characteristic of an organism that makes it suited to live or reproduce in a particular environment.

aridity A long-term lack of moisture.

Bactrian The two-humped species of camel.

biome A community of specific types of plants, animals, and other organisms that covers a large area of the Earth.

camouflage To blend in with the surroundings, especially by matching the colors or shapes of the background.

coniferous trees Trees that bear cones. Most conifers are evergreen and bear needle-shaped leaves.

desert A biome that receives less than 10 inches of rain annually.

dromedary The one-humped species of camel.

estivation A state in which the body functions of animals slow down and the animals become dormant. It is the hot-and-dry weather counterpart of hibernation.

exhale Expelling breath from the lungs.

exoskeleton The hard covering on the body of an invertebrate.

extinction The dying out of a species.

food web A diagram that shows the feeding relationships among all the different organisms in a community.

insulate To hold a steady temperature.

invertebrate An animal without a backbone.

organism Any living thing, such as a plant, an animal, a fungus, or a bacterium.

pith The central strand of spongy tissue in plants; usually functions in storage of nutrients.

playa A Spanish word that is used to designate a dry desert lake bed.

predator An animal that hunts other animals to eat them.

prey An animal that is eaten by another animal.

rain shadow An area on the leeward side of mountains on which little rain falls.

reproduction The process by which an organism creates new individuals of the same species.

species A group of animals or plants whose members can interbreed and produce fertile offspring.

stratification The layering of life zones between the peak and base of a mountain.

suction A force that attracts a substance, such as water, to an area of lesser pressure.

vertebrate An animal with a backbone.

For Further Reading

Baker, Lucy. *Life in the Deserts*. New York: Franklin Watts, 1990.

Kaplan, Elizabeth. *Taiga*. New York: Marshall Cavendish, 1996.

_____. *Temperate Forest*. New York: Marshall Cavendish, 1996.

Moore, Randy, and Vodopich, Darrell. *The Living Desert*. Hillside, NJ: Enslow, 1991.

Ricciuti, Edward R. *Fish*. Woodbridge, CT: Blackbirch Press, 1993.

_____. *Grasslands*. New York: Marshall Cavendish, 1996.

_____. *Rainforest*. New York: Marshall Cavendish, 1996.

_____. *Reptiles*. Woodbridge, CT: Blackbirch Press, 1993.

Tesar, Jenny. *Endangered Habitats*. New York: Facts On File, 1992.

_____. *Mammals*. Woodbridge, CT: Blackbirch Press, 1993.

_____. *Spiders*. Woodbridge, CT: Blackbirch Press, 1993.

Twist, Clint. *Deserts*. New York: Dillon, 1991.

Williams, Lawrence. *Deserts*. New York: Marshall Cavendish, 1990.

Index

Acknowledgments and Photo Credits
Cover: ©Richard Gorbun/Leo de Wys, Inc.; p. 6: ©Breck P. Kent/Earth Scenes; p. 11: ©Michael R. Stokios/Earth Scenes; p. 12: ©A. J. Stevens/Earth Scenes; p. 14: ©Norman Benton/Peter Arnold, Inc.; p. 15: ©John Cancalosi/Peter Arnold, Inc.; p. 16: ©Paul Erickson/Earth Scenes; pp. 19, 29, 42 (top and bottom), 54: ©C. Allan Morgan/Peter Arnold, Inc.; p. 20: ©Arthur Gloor/Earth Scenes; p. 21: ©Raymond Mendez/Earth Scenes; p. 22: ©Carlo Dani/Earth Scenes; p. 24: ©Walter H. Hodge/Peter Arnold, Inc.; p. 26: ©Ana Laura Gonzalez/Animals Animals; p. 28: ©Betty K. Bruce/Animals Animals; p. 31: ©Animals Animals; pp. 32, 38: ©Zig Leszczynski/Animals Animals; p. 35: ©Waina Cheng/Animals Animals; p. 36: ©Gerard Lacz/Animals Animals; p. 40: ©Sean Morris/Oxford Scientific Films/Animals Animals; p. 42 (middle): ©Rodger Jackman/Oxford Scientific Films/Animals Animals; p. 43: ©Matt Meadows/Peter Arnold, Inc.; p. 44: ©R. Andrew Odum/Peter Arnold, Inc.; p. 45: ©Anthony Bannister/Animals Animals; p. 47: ©Stephen Dalton/Animals Animals; pp. 48–49: ©Mike Andrews/Animals Animals; p. 50: L. L. T. Rhodes/Earth Scenes; p. 53: ©Gerald L. Kooyman/Earth Scenes; p. 57: ©Ted Levin/Animals Animals; p. 58: ©Steve Kaufman/Peter Arnold, Inc.; p. 59: ©Joe McDonald/Earth Scenes.
Artwork by Blackbirch Graphics, Inc.

00
15

JUL 1996